Northallerton

in old picture postcards volume 1

including Romanby and Brompton

by
Colin Narramore
and
Patricia Turner

European Library – Zaltbommel/Netherlands

Fourth edition: 1994

GB   ISBN 90 288 2290 9 / CIP

© 1983 European Library – Zaltbommel/Netherlands

INTRODUCTION

Northallerton is the County town and administrative centre of North Yorkshire. It owes its origins, growth and importance to its position in the centre of the Vale of York, on the main communications route between the south and the north, and as the market nucleus for a large rural area. It is thought that the Romans had a signal station on its Imperial Postal system at this spot and indeed a minor route between York and Hadrian's Wall ran close by, through what eventually became Brompton Parish. However, the town is Saxon in origin. Later in the 10th century Danish insurgents settled at Romanby and Brompton.

Its position on a major route way brought death and destruction to the town on many occasions. In 1069 the whole area was laid waste by the armies of William the Conqueror and was still waste at the time of the Domesday Book. It later suffered at the hands of the Scots in the campaign which culminated in the Battle of the Standard, fought largely in Brompton Parish in 1138, and in the later raids of the Black Douglas. During the Civil War of 1642 to 1649 the town gave shelter to King Charles I on two occasions whilst the army of the Duke of Cumberland rested there on its march to Scotland during the Jacobite Rebellion of 1745.

In the golden age of coaching Northallerton had four coaching inns along its High Street serving passengers and horses using several routes to the north. With the arrival of the railway in 1841 the town maintained its importance as a communications centre. The line from London to Edinburgh via York and Newcastle passed through the town, as did the line linking the industrial West Riding with the port and steel town of Middlesbrough.

Northallerton became by Royal Charter, the first charter was granted in 1200, the market centre for the area and also drew traders from further afield to its four annual fairs, reduced to two by the period covered in this book. Cattle drovers bringing cattle, horses and sheep from Northumbria and Scotland regularly came to the town. The original cattle market was by the Church, but sheep were sold on the High Street as late as the 1890's. With the arrival of the railway the cattle market was built close to the station, but this has subsequently closed and today a cattle market is held every Wednesday at the Applegarth.

Northallerton was a Saxon Burgh and the centre of the Wapentake of Allerton. In the Domesday Book the area is listed under the lands owned by the Bishop of Durham. William Rufus confirmed this ownership by granting to the Bishop the manorial rights, allowing the holder of the office to collect tolls and fair and market fees. The Bishop ruled the Durham Palatinate like a Prince and exercised great power. He was the Supreme Judge of the Northallerton Court Halmot and Courts Leet and Baron, but was represented by a High Steward and Deputy Steward. He had the right to appoint clergy to the churches in the area and the right of visitation, both of which were disputed for centuries by the Archbishop of York. It was this inherited dispute which caused the then Bishop of Durham, Thomas Wolsey, to order the demolition of Romanby Church in 1523. Whilst Northallerton, Romanby and Brompton are in the York Diocese, the Dean and Chapter of Durham still have the right to appoint clergy to these parishes.

The Quarter Sessions for the area were held in the town from the 17th century, in various buildings including the Tollbooth, the Guild Hall and Vine House, but eventually a Court House was built in East Road in 1785, close by a House of Correction opened in 1783.

When the Poor Law Union system was introduced, a workhouse was established in Northallerton to serve three parishes in the area. This building is now part of the Friarage Hospital. Again, when in 1856 the North Riding Constabulary was founded, one of the last County forces to be formed, Northallerton was selected as its headquarters, operating initially from premises in East Road.

With this history of local administration, Northallerton

became the obvious location for the headquarters of the North Riding County Council, and so in 1906 a purpose built structure, erected on the old racecourse to the south of the town and just within the Parish of Romanby, was opened.

Before the Reform Elections of 1832 the two Parliamentary seats for the borough were in the hands of the Lascelles family who bought the rights from the Bishop of Durham. The Reform Bill reduced the Northallerton seats to only one, widened the franchise to make eligible the solid middle class entrepreneurs and tradesmen who were becoming prominent in the town and broke the hold of the Lascelles family on the town.

The flourishing of these local business interests can be seen in the development of the railway, the growth of local industries, such as linen in Brompton, and the tarpaulin and brattice cloth factory in Northallerton, but also in a burst of civic pride and identity which led to the removal of the old shambles to be replaced with a town hall. Its position as a communication and administrative centre and as a market town led to the growth of trades and business allied to these interests, but the town has never been isolated from the mainstream of national events or wider developments in technology and social behaviour.

The period covered by the photographs reflects the town's history and its progression, from its ancient parish church, to its newer industries and businesses; from horse drawn coaches to railways and thence to the motor car. The pictures cover an exciting period of transition in the life of a town which throughout its history can be seen as a microcosm of provincial life in England.

In many ways, Romanby represents a North Yorkshire village which, because of circumstance, did not grow to become the county town or a small scale industrial village like Brompton. During the period covered by this book, Romanby remained a small settlement centred around its village green, despite the fact that it lies only a mile from the Northallerton High Street, and that the main line railway station is only a few hundred yards away from that same village green.

Roger Gale, who wrote a history of the area, put forward the idea that Romanby got its name because a Roman settlement was established there, but this is Danish in origin and in the Domesday Book it is referred to as 'Romundebi' which suggests that its origins lie in a Danish personal name, i.e. Romunds settlement. Because of its close proximity to Northallerton, the village shares the same early history of destruction and unsettled times. It had a church, but this was merely a chapel of ease attached to Northallerton Church and was dismantled in 1523. It came under the auspices of the Bishop of Durham and in 1155 the then Bishop, Hugh Pudsey, granted the tithes of the parish as an endowment to the hospital of St. James which was situated to the south of Northallerton on the road to Thirsk. This endowment continued until the 1530's when the Dissolution of the minor religious houses brought about the closure of this hospital.

The village remained without a church of its own until 1879 when the spiritual needs of the parish were recognised and the Romanby School Room was licensed for divine worship. This quickly proved to be inadequate and in 1882 a new church was built, its architect was C. Hodgson Fowler of Durham, but it was built by Thomas Wood and Company of Pickering, whilst its interior woodwork was executed by John Meynell, cabinet maker of Northallerton. The Church was dedicated to St. James, in memory of Romanby's earlier association with the St. James' hospital, by the then Archbishop of York on May 30th, 1882.

In recent years, especially since the 1960's, Romanby has expanded to meet the needs of increasing housing development in the area and is now virtually a suburb of Northallerton. However, the area around the Green remains very much unchanged and still reflects the atmosphere of an earlier, more leisurely age.

1. This picture of Northallerton in 1869 clearly shows the wide High Street, nearly half a mile in length which is typical of a Northern Yorkshire market town. Most of the buildings date from the 18th and early 19th centuries. The general roof line here depicted, remains much the same today, but the character of the High Street has been altered by the addition of modern shop fronts. The scene appears so quiet and peaceful in those days before the bustle of motor transport.

Old Northallerton. The Shambles and Cross, Main Street.

2. This postcard of 1870 shows the Tollbooth, Market Cross and Shambles which stood in the centre of the High Street. The Shambles, a double row of slaughter houses, butchers shops and tanners, had become unsightly and provided a health hazard as they attracted rats from the nearby Sun Beck. The site was purchased from the Ecclesiastical Commissioners by the Northallerton Market and Public Improvement Company and the building was demolished in 1872.

Old Northallerton, Main Street.

[handwritten message] Have you got an invite for the Whist-Drive at N. A. ... Parker Cave for 2 tickets so I expect they will be going.

3. The Tollbooth, seen here at the head of the High Street in 1870, had been at the centre of town life since before the 15th century. Here market tolls were paid to the Lord of the Manor, the Bishop of Durham and later the Ecclesiastical Commissioners. On the ground floor were several shops and over them a room where earlier the Quarter Sessions were held. The town stocks stood to the south of the building which was used as a temporary lock up. The building was purchased for £18 in 1873 and demolished, thus opening up the market place in front of the newly erected Town Hall.

4. The foundation stone for the Town Hall was laid in 1872 on the site of the old Shambles. Built in an Italianesque style of architecture by Ross of Darlington at a cost of £5,000, the building opened with a Concert Evening on December 22nd, 1873. Before its opening, Northallerton had lacked a large assembly room, but its large upper floor and stage has been in continual use for public assemblies and entertainment. The ground floor with its small shops and hall is still in use for trading and market activities, as it was in 1875 when this photograph was taken.

5. By 1904, when this picture was taken on a quiet Sunday afternoon, the Town Hall had become a prominent feature of the High Street, overlooking the wide market place. The two weekly markets, of which the Wednesday market is the oldest, have long been established. At one time there were fairs four times a year and an annual cheese fair on the second Wednesday in October, all established by a Royal Charter in the Middle Ages. There are still fairs in the Spring and Autumn when the street is filled with rides and sideshows.

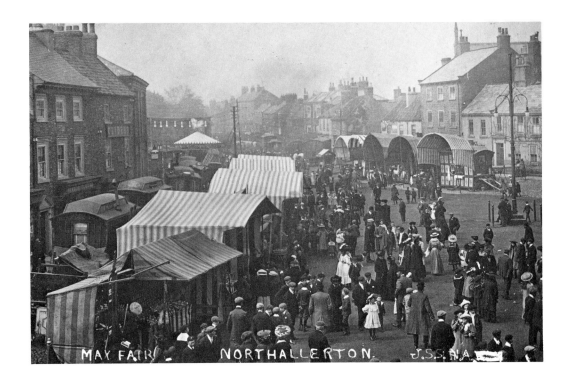

6. The Northallerton May Fair, pictured in 1920, was eagerly awaited with its noise, colour and excitement. Originally it would have been a horse and cattle fair and held by the Parish Church, but it has become more of a social entertainment, particularly in the early part of this century, the great age of the steam driven roundabouts and fair ground organs.

7. The market cross, shown here in 1922, symbolises the authority of the town to hold a market and a fair. The present cross was built in 1777, but was temporarily removed to the grounds of Mr. J.I. Jefferson at Standard House when the Shambles were demolished in 1872, but reinstalled in 1913 in its present position after the building of the Town Hall.

8. When Mr. W.R. Green, tobacconist of the High Street, used this picture in an advertisement in 1930 under the heading 'A Northallerton Oddity', he was not offering as an oddity his special Virginia Cigarettes at one shilling for twenty! The building itself did not conform the general look of the High Street, as it was the only building which presented a gable end to the street. As such it was probably the oldest building extant in that area of the town, dating from about 1650 and no doubt built upon the foundations of an even earlier structure which followed the pattern of the Saxon 'croft and toft' system of land holding.

9. The family business of J.W. Clapham, photographed here in 1910, was a large department store which specialised in drapery and clothing, where no doubt locally made linen was sold. From the pile of timber on the pavement of its High Street frontage it would appear that the premises were undergoing shop fitting alterations. The building, now with a modern plate glass facade, is still a department store, but the business is no longer owned by the Clapham family.

10. Another large emporium in the town was the Northallerton Co-operative Society, situated in the High Street. The Co-operative sold a wide range of goods, but specialised in its own brand of food products. In this picture, taken in 1927, the employees pose for a group photograph in front of the shop. They are no doubt very proud of their new motor delivery van, whose leather coated driver can be seen amongst the group. Left to right: E. Mattison, E. Pepperday, C. Pollard, L. Colley, J. Willough-by, A. Weighell, M. Burly, N. Weighell, J. Brown, H. Brown, G. Finkill, P. Ward and H. Wright.

11. In 1908, the roof of Mr. James Naylor's hardware shop in the High Street was re-tiled and the occasion marked by this photograph. Naylor and Sons sold plumber's requirements and domestic tin and galvanised iron items, but also branched out into the sale of bicycles and cyclists requisites. From repairing bicycles, the family firm moved into the newly born motor trade, becoming the first car dealers and repairers in the town. This family firm continued until a year ago, when it ceased business.

12. This impressive facade adorns the front of Barclays Bank in the High Street, pictured in 1920. Originally the Bank was a branch of the Darlington based Backhouse Bank, founded by Jonathan Backhouse, a Quaker and associate of the Pease family whose financial backing gave rise to George Stephenson's Stockton to Darlington Railway and to the development of Middlesbrough as an iron and steel manufacturing centre. The Backhouse financial interest involved itself in the development and extension of the rail network in the North East and provided Northallerton with a rail link to the ports on Teesside.

Market Place, Northallerton

13. 'The Shields Mail', the 'Edinburgh Mail', 'Hero', 'High Flyer', the 'Express' and 'Wellington', names which evoke the very spirit of travel in the stage coach days before the arrival of the railways. These coaches, which linked London with York, Leeds and Newcastle, once rattled along the High Street to deposit passengers and mail at one of the four coaching inns in the town. In this picture, taken in 1921, a reminder of these earlier days can be seen. The horse and carriage outside the Golden Lion Hotel was used to meet passengers from the railway station half a kilometre away.

Railway Station, Northallerton.

14. The railway system reached Northallerton in 1841, linking the town to the industrial West Riding and also placing it on the main line route from London to the North East and eventually Scotland. This East Coast main line was, and still is, one of the most important and fastest routes in the country. The section of track from York, through Northallerton and up to Darlington was often used as a test track on which engines and rolling stock were put through their paces. The railway gave a boost to the town. Here pictured in 1928 is the busy passenger station, a second line lead to the equally busy goods station at North End. Outside the main station the cattle pens of the auction mart were built, thus re-emphasising the town's important position as an agricultural centre.

15. Close to the railway station, to the south west of the town, was the Railway Hotel (now known as the Station Hotel), seen here in 1908 shortly after it had been enlarged and refaced in an impressive manner. As well as offering public bars and refreshment for travellers awaiting train connections to the north or south, the Station Hotel provided overnight accommodation for commercial travellers and holiday makers who arrived in the town.

South Parade, Northallerton.

16. The railway was built to the south west of the town and to link it with the High Street, the heart of Northallerton, South Parade was constructed. The houses which line it, built from 1860 onwards, were fairly large and substantial, and this area of the town seen in 1904, superseded the area around the Church as that part which attracted middle class business men, being so handy for the train, and also for business in the town. It is also very close to the County Hall building.

THE LODGE.   N⁰: ALLERTON

17. In this 1907 picture The Lodge looks like a country house but is in fact close to Thirsk Road and South Parade. The building accommodated Miss Nelson's Private School at which about twenty boys and girls between the ages of five and fifteen years were taught. Later part of the land behind the house was purchased by the newly formed Northallerton Bowling Club, whilst in later years the house was also bought by the Club, which is still in existence at these premises.

18. This garage stood at the corner of South Parade and the High Street, and was owned by Mr. Greer of Thornton-le-Beans Hall near Northallerton. It sold a wide range of motor cars, including the highly prestigious Rolls Royce. By the hand cranked petrol pump stands Mr. Pattison, the foreman, with three of his mechanics, in this picture taken in 1929. The building, which had long ceased to function as a garage, was demolished in recent years. The first motor car was seen in Northallerton on 27th November 1896.

19. The imposing building on the left of this 1875 picture is a Savings Bank and is still in use as such today. Built in 1857, it stands on an interesting site. Here stood the Guildhall where until 1720 the Quarter Sessions were held, the building then became the town workhouse, a damp unsanitary place because of its proximity to the Sun Beck. When the new Union Workhouse opened in 1857, this building was demolished and replaced by the Savings Bank.

WORKHOUSE NORTHALLERTON.

20. Changes in the Poor Law system brought about the creation in 1837 of the Northallerton Poor Law Union to cover forty parishes with an overall population of 12,460. The old workhouse proved to be inadequate, but continued in use until 1857, when a new building was erected to the east of the High Street. This could provide accommodation for one hundred and twenty-five inmates, and also casual work such as chopping firewood, sewing sacking and general duties to maintain the building in exchange for which the poor could obtain a meal. Built on land known as Friarage Fields, the site of the old Carmelite Friarage, the workhouse building later became the nucleus of the Friarage Hospital, under the local area health authority. The photograph shows the building in 1905.

21. This solid looking brick and stone building, pictured here in 1904, is the Wesleyan Methodist Chapel on the High Street close to the Rutson Hospital. Built in 1864 in the Victorian semi-gothic style, out of money raised by public subscription, and on the site of the Pack Horse Inn, it replaced an earlier Wesleyan Chapel of 1796, this older building becoming a Baptist Chapel for a time. The three stone pinnacles were later removed when they became unsafe after a severe gale. The Chapel became the centre for the Northallerton Methodist Circuit, with other member chapels in the surrounding villages.

PARISH CHURCH, NORTHALLERTON.

22. Dominating the northern area of the town is the Parish Church of All Saints. The Church was founded in the 7th century, rebuilt in stone in A.D. 885, and much enlarged between the 12th and 15th centuries as its various architectural features reveal. The Church suffered much damage in the past caused by a succession of Scottish raids on the town. The original tower, built in 1190, fell in 1318 as the result of one such sacking, and the new tower, seen in this 1922 picture, was rebuilt in 1420 in the perpendicular style. The tower contains a peal of eight bells which were recast and rehung in Victorian times.

23. This is the band of bellringers at the Parish Church, pictured in 1903. The captain of ringers, Jimmie Barnett (third left), began ringing at the age of fifteen years and only retired, with seventy years of ringing behind him in 1937. On his 66th wedding anniversary on September 1st, 1936, a flag was flown from the Church tower and Jimmie chose to mark the occasion by having himself and his wife driven all around the town by one of his ringing colleagues who was in the automobile trade. In 1900 residents living close to the Church complained about the noise on practise nights and so these were temporarily abandoned. A good bell ringing team still serves the Church in recent years the bell tower has been sound proofed. Left to right: Jim Peacock, Alf Simons, Jimmie Barnett (Captain), Jack Simons, Lawrence Brown, Harry Stevenson, Richard Shuttlesworth and unidentified.

24. A Sunday morning in 1908 and the 1st Northallerton Rifle Volunteers march from along the High Street after Church parade. This Battalion was formed as a part of the local militia during the Napoleonic Wars and was disbanded in 1908 to become part of the 4th Battalion (Territorial) of the Princess of Wales Own Yorkshire Regiment (The Green Howards).

25. A moment of poignancy is captured on this fine Summer's morning – August 6th, 1921, as this large crowd gathers by the Church to participate in the unveiling of the memorial to those young men of the town who gave their lives in the Great War of 1914-1918. Officers take the salute, the Vicar of Northallerton reads the service and speaks the oration and there can be few in the crowd who did not wipe away a tear shed in memory of a lost friend or loved one. The annual act of Remembrance is held by this memorial each year. Monies raised to provide a memorial to those who died in the 1939-1945 War was used to build a Memorial Swimming Baths, a much needed amenity.

Porch House,
Northallerton

26. This red brick, pantiled roof, house is the oldest domestic building in Northallerton. Alterations in 1844 exposed an oak beam on which were carved the initials of Richard Metcalfe and his wife and the date 1584. The Metcalfes with their seat at Nappa Hall in Wensleydale were a long established, prominent family in the area. Their coat of arms can be seen on a tombstone in the Parish Church. A staunch Royalist family in the English Civil War, the Metcalfes twice gave shelter to King Charles I in this house, firstly in August 1640 and then in 1647 when the King, then a prisoner, was being taken south by the Parliamentarians. This picture was taken in 1925, but the house remains unchanged today.

Cottage Hospital, Northallerton.

RELIABLE SERIES. N158

27. October 1877 the cottage hospital was opened in this building known as Vine House, because of the huge vine which clung to its walls. Built originally as a private dwelling, the house had been the meeting place for the Quarter Sessions between 1720 and 1770 and became the Post Office from 1850-1876. It was the only hospital in the area and financing it proved difficult until in 1890 an appeal for more subscribers brought in a succession of large donations from a Mr. John Rutson of Newby Wiske Hall and as a mark of recognition for this generosity the cottage hospital, seen here in 1904, was later named the Rutson Hospital after him. This hospital is now part of the Northallerton group of hospitals, along with the Mount and the Friarage.

28. The staff of the Rutson Hospital pose in its attractive garden in this June 1919 picture. During the First World War the hospital was mainly concerned with nursing the wounded and discharged soldiers. The Matron, Miss E.S. Osbourn, who ran the hospital from 1916 until 1929, can be seen at the centre of the group.

NORTHALLERTON.

29. This almost Scottish baronial looking building, built in 1828 and seen here in 1905, is the old vicarage, to the south of the Church, and close to Castle Hills and the town cemetary. Its size reflects the status of the vicar of Northallerton who is also the Rural Dean. The building now houses a local government department, the present vicarage being a more modest and manageable detached house in its grounds.

30. It is difficult to believe that this quiet Green at North End with its village atmosphere is only a few hundred yards beyond the bustle of the High Street. The original village of Northallerton developed here, close to the church and the long demolished castle. In this picture, taken in 1903, a group of boys play, perhaps pupils from the nearby Grammar School, in their caps, knickerbockers and eton jackets. The scene has changed very little, except for a greater flow of traffic and necessary road widening.

The Mount, Northallerton

Valentines Series

31. When this picture was taken in 1905, the Mount was a private residence owned by Mr. E. Little, a member of the cottage hospital board. It was established in 1864 as a preparatory school, run by the Reverend E. Burttleston, on a site to the north of the town where in 1138 the English Cavalry was lined up at the Battle of the Standard. It sat in extensive grounds and accommodated between forty and fifty boarders, and offered tuition for university scholarships.

32. The Little family were closely associated with the Scout and Guide movement in the Town and the Guides and Brownies had the Mount as their headquarters. This group formally poses for the camera on the front lawn in 1918. The grandchildren of many of these young girls were later to be born in the house, because it is now the Maternity Hospital, a far cry from that cavalry position of 1138!

33. This well proportioned house stands overlooking North End Green and was built in the early 19th century. Its name 'Standard House' recalls the Battle of the Standard which was fought to the north of the town in 1138. It was for many years the home of Mr. John Ingleby Jefferson, a solicitor and the Deputy Steward for the Ecclesiastical Commissioners who were Lords of the Manor of Northallerton in succession to the Bishop of Durham. Mr. Jefferson was a prominent man in the town, a solicitor and one of the management committee of the cottage hospital. It was his garden which accommodated the market cross when the Shambles was demolished and the Town Hall built in 1872-73. The house, photographed here in 1920, is now a local government office.

34. The High Street continues beyond the Town Hall, but becomes less commercial and more residential as this 1908 picture shows. This large ivy covered, double fronted house, overlooking the Church, dates from the early 19th century and was owned by William Fowle, a solicitor. For a time it was the town library, but is now local government offices. The distant stone faced three storey building is Durham House, once the Bishop of Durham's property, but now a shop.

Northallerton.

35. At the south end of the town the High Street becomes the Thirsk Road, seen here in 1913. The building to the left is the newly erected Drill Hall, built in 1911 at a cost of £2,200 and was the headquarters of the 4th Battalion (Territorial) Alexandra, Princess of Wales' Own Yorkshire Regiment. Raised as a foot regiment in 1688 and known as the Green Howards, it became associated with Yorkshire in 1782 when it became the first North Riding Regiment. It became the Princess of Wales' Own Regiment in 1875 when the Princess, later Queen Alexandra, presented it with new colours. On the outbreak of war in 1914 this local Territorial Battalion was quickly drawn into action in Belgium. Today the Drill Hall is the headquarters of the Army cadet force and the local Army Careers Office.

36. A Grammar School was founded in the town in 1327, to teach church and choral music as well as Latin and Greek. The Bishop of Durham endowed it with a scholarship worth £10 per year, to Peterhouse College, Cambridge. It occupied a building close to the church, which was rebuilt in the 18th century. In 1909 a new Grammar School was built amidst spacious playing fields to the south east of the High Street. The master of the 1327 Grammar School was John Podefay, but here in 1912 the pupils of the new school pose in a group with their headmaster, John William Bearder, M.A., Ph.D.

51378. NORTHALLERTON. GRAMMAR SCHOOL.

37. When this picture was taken in 1916, the Great War had been raging for two years and the Grammar School had been requisitioned as an Army Centre housing men of the Yorkshire Regiment (Green Howards). Hence the flag pole and the two field guns mounted outside the main block on the spot where the pupils posed for that 1912 group photograph. During the War, rooms were set aside at County Hall, where the pupils received their lessons until 1918.

OAK MOUNT NORTHALLERTON.

38. This 1906 picture of Oak Mount which lies on the Thirsk Road was built in 1902 as the residence of Mr. J. Walker, the owner of North Arch Tannery in Northallerton and the Egglescliffe Tannery at Yarm, the business being established in 1861. These tanneries prepared oak bark, tanned shaved and dressed hides, curried harness and bridle leather. Tanning was long associated with the town, some tanners operating in the old shamble buildings. The house is now an old people's home.

COUNTY HALL NORTHALLERTON.

39. Northallerton was historically the centre of administration for the North Riding of Yorkshire, so with the development of the Local Government system in the late 19th century it became the natural choice for the headquarters of the North Riding County Council. By the beginning of the 20th century it was obvious that the older buildings in East Road and Zetland Street were inadequate and so plans were made for a new building on the site of the old racecourse, close to the railway station. Work on the new headquarters, which were to cost £25,000, began in 1903 and the building was not opened until January 1906. This picture, taken late in 1905, shows the main administrative block, builders materials can be seen where now there are lawns and flower beds.

The New Police Station, Northallerton.

40. The North Riding Constabulary was established in 1856 with a Chief Constable and fifty men, and a headquarters in East Road, Northallerton, close to the Prison and Magistrates Court. By 1908 these premises had become inadequate and so a new police headquarters was built in Racecourse Lane, close to County Hall, and opened in 1910 when this picture was taken. This building continued as the headquarters of the North Yorkshire Police until 1977 by which time it too had become overcrowded. Newby Wiske Hall was purchased from the Rutson family to become the new headquarters, whilst this building in Racecourse Lane became the Town Police Station.

41. Early in the 18th century the first Fire Station was opened on Fosters Yard (now part of Northallerton Co-operative). Towards the end of the 19th century, it was found that certain insurance companies would not insure property in the town against the risk of fire unless more up-to-date fire fighting equipment was made available. A horse-drawn Merryweather steam fire engine was purchased about 1890 and a number of the gentlemen formed the Brigade. The first fire attended after the purchase of the steamer was on a Christmas morning at Solberge Hall; no arrangements had been made for horses to tow the appliance and, therefore, it was man-handled by the firemen the four and a half miles to the Hall from Northallerton. Unfortunately not one of the firemen knew how to operate this new piece of equipment and it had to stand by whilst the Hall was completely burned out. The photograph, taken in 1899, shows the Brigade outside their headquarters on East Road. Left to right: J. Guthrie (Currier); G.J. Robinson (Insurance Agent); G. Eyre (Grocer); Dr. Barton (Vicar); Dr. Tweedie (Doctor); R. Prest (Shopkeeper); A. Robinson (Printer); Mr. Nettleton (Vet); J. Ward (Draper); H. Ward (Civil Servant); R. Bell (Solicitor); Mr. Smith (Ironmonger) and J. Dale (Proprietor of Golden Lion).

42. The town was served by its own newspaper, 'The North Riding and Northallerton News', printed in the town from 1900-1927 and appearing weekly every Saturday. Here, in 1908, the staff pose for the camera with the newspaper's proprietor, Mr. Joseph Carlill Savill, seen here with his bowler hat on his knee. The young man at the right of the picture is the compiler's maternal grandfather. The newspaper included items of national news as well as local stories.

FATAL AEROPLANE WRECK NEAR NORTHALLERTON. 15.5.14. J.S.S. 2.

43. One of the items which the 'North Riding and Northallerton News' must have featured in May 1914 was the crash of a Royal Flying Corps aircraft of No. 2 Squadron, to the north of the town. This type 10 B.E. Biplane had taken an early morning flight from Seaton Carew in County Durham, when it hit dense fog and the pilot attempted a landing with disasterous results. The pilot and his mechanic were both killed. Aeroplanes were still a novelty and so this accident aroused tremendous curiosity and a Question asked in Parliament. During the Great War there were several landing fields in the area of the town, whilst in the Second World War the town became a centre for off duty Bomber Command personnel, and in the later stages these were mainly Canadians.

44. The local paper no doubt gave publicity to this Belgian flag day held in the town in August 1915. During the Great War many Belgian children were billeted in the area 'for the duration', both in Northallerton and the surrounding villages. There appears to have been close links with that country. In 1820 a younger son of the Wilford family went to Belgium and founded a linen manufacturing industry at Famise, a business which continued long after the linen manufacturing in the Northallerton area ceased. There was an exchange of ideas and linen technology between Belgium and the Northallerton area, hence Northallerton's special interest in raising funds for Belgium by a flag day.

45. Carnival time provides a great opportunity for people to assume fancy dress and parade through the town. These ladies, a gay assortment of gipsies, geisha girls and victorian matrons, line up, with their suitably bedecked bicycles, to await judging at the 1910 Carnival, watched by a group of critical spectators. The carnival has been revived in recent years, but it perhaps lacks the gay, holiday atmosphere of this earlier event.

46. The British National Brass Band competition is nowadays held at the Royal Albert Hall in London, but for many years it was staged in the open air at Hardraw Falls in Wensleydale. During the competitions Northallerton railway station would bustle with passengers arriving from all parts of the country, in order to board the special trains which would take them to that picturesque Dales venue. Brass Bands have had a long association with the north of England. Northallerton, along with most northern towns, had its own Brass Band. The ensemble (Northallerton Borough Band) pictured here in 1875 won second prize in the Darlington Silver Band competition of that year, a competition which was one of the heats in the national competition. Back row, left to right: T. Jenkinson, H. Daughty, A. Barker, J. Barker, E. Thompson, E. Stockhill, F. Fowler, R. Weighell and J. Marwood. Front row, left to right: J. Meynell, C. Fowler, H. Lumley, G. Curry, J. Barnett, P. Neal and R. Shuttlesworth.

47. In 1899 the Northallerton Electric Light and Power Company was founded by a Mr. Ernest Hutton. Here, in 1920, a new underground electricity cable is being laid along Romanby Road to the Linoleum Factory and Mr. Fawcett and his gang of cable layers pose for the camera to record this event.

48. 'I want all you lads in early tomorrow for a formal works photograph', was the edict which went out, from Mr. Thomas Place, timber merchant, one day in 1900. Messrs. T. Place and Sons started from small beginnings in 1890 in a yard at North End. At its height the company employed eighty men. Most of the timber came from large estates in the area and was cut to supply shipyards, collieries and local builders in Place's extensive timber yards. The Forestry Commission has since planted and manages large forests in the nearby Cleveland and Hambleton Hills at Ingleby, Osmotherley and Boltby.

49. August 9th, 1928, Viscount Lascelles lays the foundation stone of Church House in Romanby Road. This building was used for Parish meetings and functions. Viscount Lascelles was the husband of the Princess Royal and in 1929 he succeeded his father as 6th Earl of Harewood. The Lascelles family were long associated with the area, holding lands in Brompton and Northallerton, and also controlling the two Northallerton Parliamentary seats until the Reform Elections of 1832. Lascelles Lane and the Harewood Arms in the town are current reminders of this association.

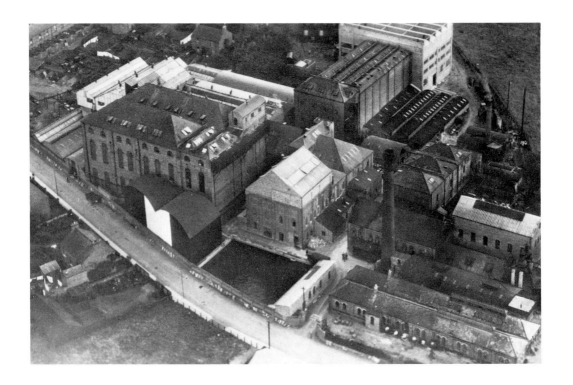

50. The chief factory in the town was the Northallerton Linoleum Company, which belonged to Messrs. Miles, Sykes and Company Limited, who bought the business in 1912. The business was founded in the mid-19th century by Sir George Elliott, M.P. for Northallerton, but originally made only tarpaulin and brattice cloth. The new owners introduced the manufacturing of linoleum, harness, horse cloths and motor car covers. In 1922, when this picture was taken, it employed about two hundred workers.

Council School, Northallerton.

51. By the early years of this century it was realised that the National School in East Road was too small for the growing population of the town, and that a new Infant School was needed. After much controversy concerning the site of this new school, building began in Springwell Lane in March 1908. The school, to be called the Applegarth, was opened in 1909. This picture shows the building in 1925.

52. These children are having a singing lesson with their teacher, Miss Harrison, in 1911. This large hall lies at the centre of the building, surrounded by the classrooms, one of which can be seen through the glass screens in the background. Built at a cost of £4,329.8s.6d. by Rhodes of Leeds, the school reflects the style of architecture of the time. The interior is exactly the same today, apart from improvements in the heating and lighting.

ROMANBY CHURCH.

53. A Church had existed in Romanby since medieval times as a Chapel of Ease for Northallerton Church, but this was demolished in the 1520's on the orders of Cardinal Wolsey when the Vicar refused to comply with his wishes. In 1879 the Romanby School room was licensed for divine worship and an additional curate was appointed. However, this proved to be inadequate and in June 1881 the foundation stone for St. James' Church was laid by Mr. John Hutton of Solberge Hall, a local landowner. The new Church was consecrated by the Archbishop of York on May 30th, 1882. The picture shows the Church in 1904.

54. A peaceful summer's day by the Green at Romanby in 1903. Two boys, one in Norfolk jacket, knickerbockers and cloth cap, the other in a sailor suit, reflect the fashion in children's dress at the beginning of the century as they carry home milk pails. The cottages show a mixture of domestic architectural styles, the earliest dating from the mid-18th century.

55. The Golden Lion Inn at Romanby faces onto the Green and is here seen as it was in the 1880's, when it offered not only ale, but also stabling for horses. The building has been much altered as the photograph evidences. New bricks on the gable end show an alteration in the roof line. The gently bowed windows would have been installed in the early 18th century, whilst the angular bay beneath the Inn sign would be a more recent addition. Evidence of bricked up doorways beyond that bay reveal that this part of the building had been a row of cottages.

Romanby, Northallerton.

56. By 1913, when this picture was taken, the Golden Lion had been further altered. The roof on the farthest part of the building had been raised to produce a more regular roof line. The curved bays had been replaced by larger more angular bays, one of which extended well onto the pavement, and the upstairs sash windows had been replaced with casements. The horse being led into the street would suggest that the Inn still offered good stabling. Looking at this rural scene, it is hard to believe that the busy main railway line runs just behind the row of cottages across the Green or that Northallerton Railway Station is only a few hundred yards away from the Golden Lion Inn.

Romanby War Memorial

57. This splendid clock tower stands to the south of Romanby Green on the Ainderby Road and is a memorial to those men of the Parish who died in the 1914-1918 War. By the time that this picture was taken, in 1927, housing development in the village had extended beyond the Green and was to further expand in the inter-war years. More recent building has greatly increased the size of the village, so that it is difficult to identify Romanby as a community distinct from Northallerton. Only the area around the Green remains unspoilt and unchanged.

Brompton

The village of Brompton lies one and a half miles to the north of Northallerton. Like Northallerton it was originally an Anglo-Saxon settlement and was listed in the Domesday Book under the land belonging to the Bishop of Durham. In the 10th and early 11th centuries the village was under Anglo-Danish occupation as is evidenced by the rare 'hogback' sculptures of that period, which were discovered embedded in the Church fabric during extensive restoration in 1868.

Brompton owes its existence to the Willow Beck which flows through the village and into Northallerton to join eventually with the river Wiske. Its course has determined the development of the settlement; its water has provided power for the linen mills and has been the means of recreational pursuits, including boating and skating in due season. The village developed historically into two distinctive areas, each with its own character. Nearest to Northallerton is High End, which is centred on the Church and its triangular Green. At its northern end a crossroad was formed by the Northallerton and Bullamoor to Lazenby roads. Beyond this and over a slight ridge of land, known as Cockpit Hill, lies the second area,

Water End, which from Danish derived place names, associated with this part of the village, probably represents the Danish settlement in Brompton. Water End is characterised by the wide Green on each side of the Willow Beck, bordered by rows of cottages. In both areas the medieval 'croft and toft' layout can still be traced despite subsequent centuries of housing development which has superseded this pattern of land holding.

The period covered by the pictures, was the height of the linen manufacturing industry in the village. Linen had been produced in the home since the early 18th century, but this was organised on a commercial basis using the 'putting out' system by several entrepreneurs of which John Wilford and John Pattison were the most enterprising. It was they who, with other local business interests, agitated for the extension of a railway line which would link Brompton with the ports at Teesside and the textile centre of Leeds. Over two decades of dispute were to pass until eventually their persistence lead to the opening of the railway branch line in 1854. Now that the cheap transportation of cheap coal and raw flax was established, the linen industry could develop into a factory system with steam powered machines, using water from the Beck. This development, coming late as it did, meant that the industry grew on steady foundations in the village, long after speculative investment and the post Napoleonic Wars had seen the decline of the industry in other areas.

The linen industry brought wealth to the village and not just to the mill owners who occupied the larger houses. From the 1800's onwards new workers cottages were built around High End Green and at Water End; money was raised to restore the Church and the Methodist Chapels; a Mechanics Institute was founded; football and cricket teams were formed together with a bowls and tennis club. The village sported an Orchestra and a Brass Band and other recreational pursuits were met by the Allotment Society, Temperance meetings and dancing classes, held in the Oddfellows Hall which was purchased by Mr. Todd of Mill Hill in the 1930's and presented to the village to be used as a Village Hall. The village, with a population of about 1,700, supported six public houses and eighteen shops. Trades directories over this period show the introduction of new trades like bicycle, and later, car repairing. In the early part of this century a dozen or so of the more prominent Brompton residents became subscribers to the telephone system. Motor cars and telegraph poles begin to feature in pictures taken in the latter part of the period covered.

For a brief period from the beginning of the century until the Great War of 1914-1918, the village attracted day trippers from Teesside during the Summer months. The carnival and sports in early June was a great attraction and still is. For several seasons the Beck at Water End was dammed to form a boating lake, where boats could be hired at 1d. and 2d. per hour. One enterprising shopkeeper commissioned souvenir china depicting a Brompton 'Coat of Arms' for sale to the visitors who arrived by train from industrial Middlesbrough, Stockton and Darlington.

The Great War brought an end to these activities. The development of man-made fibres produced a decline in the linen industry and both of the village factories closed in the early 1960's. However, this boom period, depicted in the pictures, has left many tangible marks upon the physical appearance and character of the village.

58. In 1908 the road which links Northallerton to Brompton was unmetalled with only the Vicarage and the Wesley Manse beside it until the village centre was reached. To the left were allotment plots whilst to the right were the grounds of Mill Hill House, built by Mr. Herbert Wilford, part of which were given to the village by a subsequent owner, to be used as a Recreation Ground. The Church tower and the chimney of the Wilford Mill can be seen to the left. The road leads directly onto High End Green and the crossroads beyond.

59. Northallerton Road in 1930 is by then surfaced with pavements on both sides at this spot by the Church Hall. This building with its little steeple was built in 1875, the porch added in 1922. Here the Church Sunday School met and in the winter months church services were held because its cast iron coal burning stove gave a warmth and comfort which the unheated Church could not provide.

60. The Northallerton Road climbs up the hill from the High End with the Wesley Manse at the crown. The cottages to the left date from the late 18th century and beyond the row the little steeple on the Church Hall can be seen above the roofs. The row of houses to the right, with the corner shop, and known as Primrose Terrace, were built in the 1870's. The novelty of a man with a camera attracted the curious who were only too willing to pose, as these children did in 1924.

61. The imposing house seen in 1914 to the right of the picture stands on the High Green and dates from the mid-18th century. For a few years in the 1840's it housed the first vicar of the Parish, Reverend John Middleton, until a vicarage was built on Northallerton Road. By this house were two cottages used to provide shelter for cattle drovers who passed through the village driving beasts from the Border regions to the markets of the industrial North and Midlands. The pinfold where the cattle were kept for the night was a fenced off area of the Green behind the house. A village lock up, built in 1825, adjoined the cottages and the Pinfold.

62. Until 1912 the Old Tolbooth stood in the centre of the Brompton crossroads. In its latter days part of it housed a 'fish and chip' shop whilst the remainder was rented to Messrs. Walker who stored their coal wagons there. The building was a focal point; a meeting place for gossip and where children played ball games against its walls. It was purchased by Mr. Claude Wilford for £200 and immediately demolished because he regarded it as an obstruction to the new 'motor' traffic which was becoming increasingly popular. This area of the village, seen here in 1910, is still called 'Shop End' by the inhabitants.

63. This picture, taken in 1919, shows Church Green as seen from the crossroads, the view opened up by the removal of the Tollbooth in 1912. The cottages facing onto the Green reflect the medieval plan of the village. The view is softened and enhanced by the maturing trees around the Green, mainly Horse Chestnuts, which are the centre of attention of the children during the 'conker' season in the Autumn.

64. In 1906 there were eighteen shops in Brompton, not including the Post Office and several 'fish and chip' shops. Walker and Son ran a general store and were also coal merchants. At weekends and on holidays the horse-drawn coal wagons were cleaned and used to carry passengers on excursions to the moors. From this developed Walker's motor coach business, which remained in family hands until recently. Fawcett's grocery shop can be seen further along the row. Its owner commissioned souvenir china with a Brompton 'Coat of Arms' on it, which was sold to day-trippers who visited before the Great War.

65. The road over Cockpit Hill links the High Green with Water End and has altered little since this 1906 picture. The corner by the Three Horse Shoes public house made a good meeting place for the men and boys of the village. Next to it is the then recently opened Co-operative Society shop, whilst on the crown of the hill stands the Oddfellows Hall, the scene of many village socials. The chimney in the distance towers above Sherwood's corn mill, now converted into houses.

BROMPTON NORTHALLERTON

THE "STEVEN" SERIES

66. The Willow Beck flows through the village and is the central feature of the area known as Water End. This 1908 picture shows the Ford and lower footbridge. In 1912 Claude Wilford financed the building of a road bridge at this spot which would enable him to drive his motor car to his house without the need to drive through the ford. Mr. Wilford, a mill owner and a prominent local figure, was the first car owner in the village.

67. An almost continuous row of cottages lines the eastern side of the Willow Beck at Water End, pictured here in 1912. When the village was enclosed in the 18th century, the existing tenants at Water End were given grazing rights on the green's alongside the Willow Beck, and in the early part of the 20th century, most cottagers kept geese which were allowed to wander freely. In the early days of the linen industry in the village, some cottagers built loom sheds on the long strips of land behind their cottages, whilst others had hand looms in the front rooms of their homes.

68. Before the First World War, the industrial workers of Middlesbrough and Stockton would travel by train for a day trip to Brompton, in the Summer months. The Willow Beck at Water End would be dammed to create a boating lake, and rowing boats could be hired by the hour. A familiar sight, pictured here in 1914, are a flock of geese together with two of the rowing boats which were destined to be broken up for fuel during the Great War. One Summer a Circus came to Water End and elephants grazed by the Willow Beck.

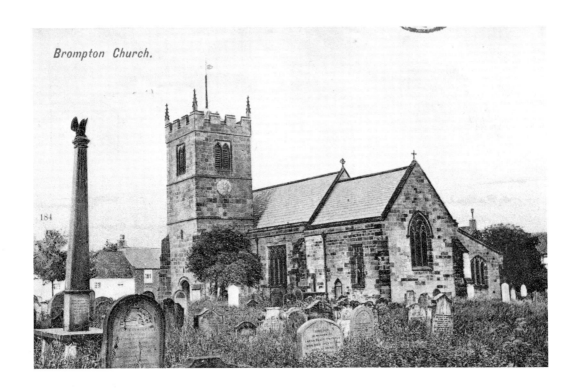

Brompton Church.

69. A Church existed in the village in Saxon times, but was rebuilt in sandstone and evolved into its present plan between the 12th and 15th centuries. In 1868 extensive restoration was carried out, during which the 'Hogback' sculptures, dating from the Viking occupation, were discovered in the walls of the Chancel, together with fragments of Saxon crosses, which are now displayed in the Church. The exterior was refaced in 1868, but still the Church presents a timeless quality as the focal point of the Church Green, as it does here in 1905.

BROMPTON CHURCH INTERIOR. NO. 2377.

70. This interior picture of the Church, taken in 1925, shows the results of the 1868 restoration, which swept away the galleries and box pews of an earlier fashion and replaced them with a Victorian expression of Church decoration, the stained glass, the pitch pine pews, and pulpit, the stone font and the Biblical texts. More recent redecoration has brought about alterations to the Sanctuary and removed the Biblical texts, but the basic details can still be easily identified today.

HIGH END, BROMPTON.

71. The large building seen to the left of High Green in 1915 was the Wesleyan Methodist Chapel, built in 1817 and restored in 1878. John Wesley preached many times at Northallerton and Osmotherley, and one of the first Chapel Trustees was the linen manufacturer John Wilford. The Chapel is now the Scout headquarters. In 1893 the Chapel Sunday School was built and can be seen in the distance. The large houses on either side of the Chapel were the homes of two members of the Yeoman family of linen manufacturers, who inherited the Pattison Mill.

72. The Primitive Methodist Chapel, now a private house, was erected on Cockpit Hill, in 1821. Its minister in 1906, Reverend G.J. Lane, is pictured here with chapel officials. After the Primitive and Wesleyan Methodists amalgamated in 1934, the former Wesleyan Sunday School was used as the Methodist Chapel and for many years afterwards this building was used as a Sunday School.

73. A school existed in the village since 1840. This was taken over as a Board school under the 1870 Education Act and was later enlarged to become the building seen in this postcard of 1906. The building served the educational needs of the village at a Primary level until 1974, when it was demolished and replaced with a modern open plan building with a nursery unit to accommodate children from three and a half years upwards. Village children receive their Secondary education at the two-tiered comprehensive school in Northallerton.

74. These pupils in class two of Brompton School, with their teacher Mrs. Jane Brown, faced the camera in 1890. Their formal education ended at twelve years and comprised a basic grounding in reading, writing and arithmetic, with religious instruction and needlework as the only extra's. However, the school prided itself on its singing and frequently won first prize in the local School Choral Festival held in Northallerton. One or two children in the senior year managed to gain scholarships to the Grammar School in Northallerton and thus extended their formal education.

75. This uniformed and bemedalled gentleman is P.C. George Tiffany, the Brompton Village 'Bobby', pictured in 1912, outside his house at Water End. He was responsible for policing the village, travelling over his Parish beat on his bicycle in the days when community policing was the pattern of law reinforcement in the country. A stern word, or a timely 'clip round the ear' from him was often all that was needed to pull wrongdoer's into line and as such his word and authority was well respected.

76. In 1846 an Act of Parliament authorised the building of the Yarm branch of the Leeds and Thirsk Railway Company to link Leeds with Teesside after years of discussion between the local business interest who supported it, and the landed interests who did not. Building started in 1852, mainly undertaken by Irish navies and by the time the line opened on May 15th, 1854, the original Company had been taken over by the North Eastern Railway. For many years earlier this century the Sunday Schools would join together and hire a train to take scholars and parents for a day excursion to the sea at Redcar. The railway station, pictured in 1922, was closed to passenger transport in the 1960's.

77. The manufacture of linen began in the village in the 1750's and for over a century was carried out by weavers working at home on hand looms which dominated the main room in the cottages. A few weavers continued to work at home up to the early years of this century. This picture, taken in 1912, shows a row of weavers cottages by the Church yard, built in the typical architecture of artisans houses in the area, and dating from the 1750's.

78. The two linen factories were built in the late 1850's, when the opening of the railway line through the village made the transportation of coal and raw flax much cheaper. Steam power looms were driven by water drawn from the Willow Beck which flows beneath the engine room of the Pattison Yeoman Mill, shown in this picture of 1904. Beyond is the Wilford Mill, built close to the coalyard. Both Mills were closed in the early 1960's, when the demand for linen was superseded by the cheaper man-made fabrics.

79. In this group photograph of 1888, Mr. Claude Wilford poses with a foreman, a mechanic and the female loom minders and bobbin winders at his factory. Children left school at twelve years of age and for the girls the mill provided alternative employment to domestic service or work on the land. After marriage and child bearing many women returned to the mill, especially in the peak period of production from 1890-1914.

80. Brompton mills produced three types of linen cloth, sheeting, huckaback towelling and heavy suiting. The latter provided tropical uniforms for the Army in India and was also exported to South America. Those ladies, pictured in the weaving shop in 1910, are loom minders; behind them are racks of bobbins to replace those in use on the looms. The men set up the looms supervised the various departments and maintained the machines. The working day started at 6.00 a.m. and ended at 5.00 p.m. with breaks for breakfast and lunch, the beginning and end of each break signalled by a distinctive hooter or klaxon. The weaving shop was a noisy place of work, but the weavers were almost the 'aristocracy' of the textile industry. From left to right: Minnie Mitchinson, Polly Wright, Hilda Parker, Meg Blackburn, Ada Brown, Mrs. Coltman and George Robinson.

81. Each bale of linen was inspected before it was dispatched. These workers, pictured in 1910, had a high standard to maintain. Brompton linen was represented at the Great Exhibition and the Paris Exhibition and won medals on each occasion. The linen industry absorbed most of the working population apart from those working in agriculture and it brought a certain degree of wealth and expansion to the village.

82. All the larger houses in the village were built by members of the two mill owning families, between 1750 and the early twentieth century: Manor House, Cedar Mount, Mill Hill and The Close. John Pattison Yeoman lived in the Close and it is photographed here in 1930. On its lawn the Northallerton Operatic Society gave a performance of H.M.S. Pinafore in the 1920's. The Yeoman family were prominent in local affairs as Justices of the Peace, school governors, church wardens and patrons of the arts. The house is now a children's home.

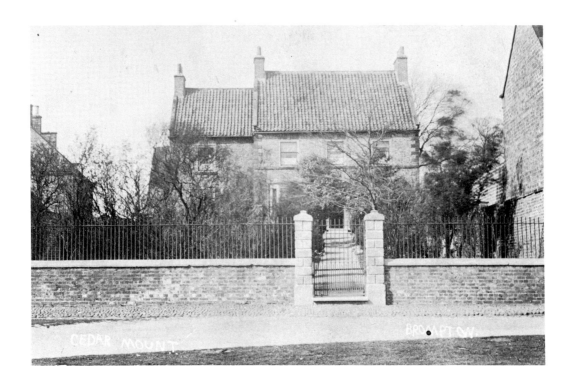

83. Cedar Mount at Water End, pictured in 1905, was the home of Claude Wilford, great-grandson of the founder of the family linen business. Built in the late 18th century in local materials, the house reflects the solid middle class values of the entrepeneur in the early Industrial Revolution, Claude Wilford was the last of the family to be involved in the business and it was only a few years after his death that linen production in the village ceased.

BROMPTON 14

84. The top of the Church Tower provides a good vantage point for viewing the children's Whitsuntide Sports on Church Green as this 1913 picture shows. The Brompton carnival and sports has altered in character to suit changes in taste and fashion, but still includes the fancy dress procession and children's sports. Nowadays a fair, with thrilling rides and sideshows, is held on the spot where these children of an earlier generation gathered together for races and sports.

85. The origins of the Whitsuntide Sports in Brompton are way beyond the memory of even the oldest inhabitants. The carnival procession is a feature which still draws large crowds of people. This carnival float of 1928, a flat deck cart pulled by a magnificently bedecked shire horse, used everyday on more mundane tasks on the farm, reflects a patriotic theme of the time and won the Masterman Cottage Challenge Cup, donated at the beginning of the century by Mrs. C.M. Masterman, the wife of a prominent landowner, which is still presented to the best float in the carnival each year.

The Brompton Orchestra.

86. The musicians in this picture, taken on High Green in 1912, are members of the Brompton Orchestra. A contemporary newspaper item gives report of a Bachelor's Social evening held at the Oddfellows Hall at which this popular orchestra presented a concert and then provided 'sprightly' music for the dancing that followed. During the winter months entertainment of this nature was well supported and the orchestra provided music for the weekly dancing classes held in the Oddfellows Hall.

87. Before the Great War there were three football teams in the village playing in different leagues, and each one regularly becoming league champions at the end of the season. The 1912 team, here shown, won both the Allertonshire League and the Milbank Charity Cup. The previous year the teams inside right, Neesam, was signed to play for Grangetown in the Northern League. Several of these young men were to lose their lives in the War. Of recent years the Brompton football team has been revived and maintains the high standards set by these proud lads.

Battle of the Standard Memorial, Northallerton

88. Despite its long history, Brompton has only appeared on the pages of our national history on one occasion. On August 22nd, 1138, the Battle of the Standard, between the English and the Scots, was fought within the parish, just to the north of the village settlement. The Scots suffered heavy losses: hundreds of their dead were buried along the line of a later bridle path known as Scot Pits Lane. This lane and Standard Hill farm were the only means of recalling the Battle until the erection of the monument on the Darlington Road to the west of the village in 1910 by public subscription at a cost of £26.18s.0d.